The Girl Who Blamed the World

By Cindy M.

Illustrated by Shirley Chiang

Published in the United States of America by:
Cyrano Books
918 12th avenue suite 1000
Honolulu, HI 96816

ISBN: 978-0-9990993-3-9

www.cyranobooks.com

For:
Hannah, Albert, Sophie
Emma, Leo and Paige

Rosa Lee was a girl who blamed the world
for her wonky eye, her frizzy curls
AND for all the things that weren't so great.....

...like losing a game for stealing home plate.

3

"Why me?" she'd shout. "Why not him?
Why do I lose
    when he gets to win?"

4

She sat with a huff, pressed her nose to her knee
and said with a scowl, "Woe is me."

When Rosa was six she blamed the world
for her wonky eye, her frizzy curls
AND for her friend who broke her dolly's head,
stuck her finger in the pudding, then wet the bed.

"Why can SHE play with my food?
Why can SHE be a pest?
Why do I have to host some creature called a GUEST?"

She sat with a huff,
    pressed her nose to her knee
and said most foul, "Woe is me."

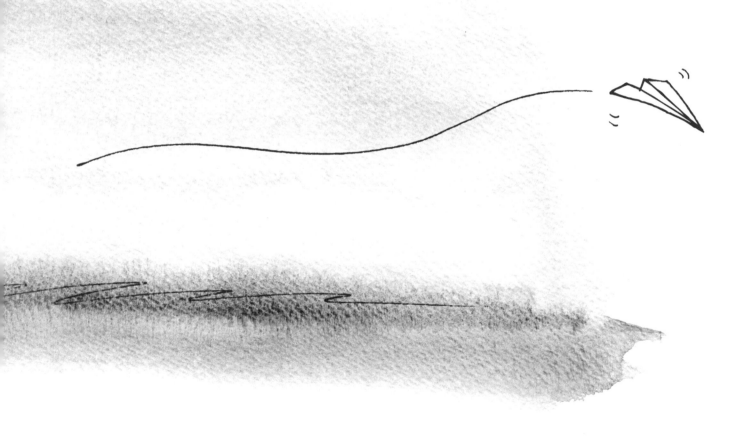

When Rosa was ten she blamed the world
for her wonky eye, her frizzy curls
AND for her brother who was a shelter to fleas,
blew his nose on the towels,
and STILL got ALL the gifts under the tree.

"Why does he get away with murder
when I get the blame?
If favoritism were a crime, you'd SURELY all be DETAINED!"

She sat with a huff, pressed her nose to her knee and said with a howl, "Woe is me."

12

At thirteen Rosa blamed the world
for her wonky eye, her frizzy curls
AND for her Father, the Tyrant of Needless Chores,
who cancelled her allowance
when she wouldn't clean the kitchen floor.

"Why can't I GET without having to
GIVE and GIVE and GIVE?
Show me a planet with no-strings-attached!
Because THAT'S where I'D like to live!"

She sat with a huff, pressed her nose to her knee
and said with a yowl, "Woe is me."

When she was fifteen Rosa blamed the world
for her wonky eye, her frizzy curls
AND for her teacher who required near perfection
in reading, writing, and scientific experimentation.

"Why do you expect so much of me?
We teenagers are very frail!
Don't you know if you set the bar too high,
we are certainly certain to fail?"

19

She sat with a huff, pressed her nose to her knee
and said with a growl, "Woe is me."

At seventeen Rosa blamed the world
for her wonky eye, her frizzy curls
AND for her Mother, the Queen of Insufferable Prudes,
who sent Rosa to the dungeon
for expressing herself with food.

"Why can't I be who I am without being punished
NIGHT after NIGHT?
If this truly is a free country,
why do YOU get to tell me who's WRONG and who's RIGHT?"

24

She sat with a huff, pressed her nose to her knee and repeated her vow, "Woe is me."

At twenty-two Rosa blamed the world
for her wonky eye, her frizzy curls
AND for her boss who was so full of greed
that he never raised her salary
even when she begged, "pretty please?"

"Why does HE have so MUCH when I have so LITTLE?
I shouldn't have to struggle and toil
just to live a life in the MIDDLE!"

She sat with a huff, pressed her nose to her knee
and scrunched her brow, "Woe is me."

When she was forty-six Rosa blamed the world
for her wonky eye, her frizzy curls
AND for a life that felt empty and void
despite the birth of the triplets:

Hannah, Hazel and Boyd.

"Why am I stranded when everyone is at sea?
If I had no obligations, I could explore the Great Yangtze!"

She sat with a huff, pressed her nose to her knee
and threw in the towel, "Woe is me."

Years later at ninety-three...
Rosa blamed the world
for her wonky eye, her frizzy curls
AND for her body so weak and pale
she couldn't do the simplest things
like bake a cake or get the mail.

"What have I done to fail life's test?
I surely deserve more than YOU and YOU and ALL THE REST!"

Arrrgghh ......

She sat with a huff, pressed her nose to her knee
and wiggled her jowl, "Woe is me."

Just as she let out a sigh of defeat,
Rosa Lee heard a voice that was oh so soft -
...and oh so sweet.

She raised her head to see her grandson at her chair
with a smile on his face and a hand full of pear.

He said, "Don't be sad, Grandma!
   It is a CHOICE to remain forever blue.

Happiness isn't a given, after all,
but the RIGHT TO PURSUE IT
   is what is guaranteed to me and you."

42

43

The End.

44

CPSIA information can be obtained
at www.ICGtesting.com
Printed in the USA
LVHW010259160519
618040LV00002B/7/P